A SMILE
A CHUCKLE
OR
A LOUD GUFFAW

OR
WHAT HAPPENED WHEN
I WASN'T LOOKING?

HUMOROUS POEMS ABOUT
SENIOR CITIZENS
BY
MARGUERITE LOUCKS DYE

Published in the United States of America by
Armadillo Poetry Press
P.O. Box 3184, St. Augustine, FL 32085-3184
(904) 794-0294

Enjoy !

Marguerite Loucks Dye

1.

ACKNOWLEDGEMENTS

Nancy Levins for her help and encouragement.

My family and friends for laughing at my poems and
urging me onward and upward.

My wonderful husband, Willard, for his patience
and his cheerful proof-reading.

MARGUERITE LOUCKS DYE is a member of The
Manatee Writers' Guild, The Manatee Poetry Group,
Night Owls, Writers' Workshop (of REAP), The League
of Vermont Writers, New England Writers and The
National League of American Pen Women (the Sarasota,
Florida and Southern Vermont branches.)

Her poems are in numerous Humorous Anthologies,
Poetry Class Chapbooks, and they have been published in
many newsletters, newspapers and Journals.

She has been a CONTRIBUTING WRITER for THE
MOUNTAIN TIMES, Killington, Vermont.

She thoroughly enjoys reading her poetry to groups large
and small, and hearing the laughter.

A DAY WITHOUT LAUGHTER IS A DAY WASTED

LAUGHTER IS MEDICINE FOR THE SOUL

A SMILE, A CHUCKLE, OR A LOUD GUFFAW

OR

WHAT HAPPENED WHEN I WASN'T LOOKING?

BY

MARGUERITE LOUCKS DYE

MARGUERITE LOUCKS DYE was born in South Dakota and lived there until she left for college – Northwestern University, two years, and The University of Minnesota, two years – a Music Major. "I've taught piano since I was in Junior High School." Her father was a well known lawyer (Speaker of The House of Representatives, South Dakota) and her mother was a poet and artist. Bill is "my fantastic brother."

She and her husband, Willard, lived in many places before spending thirty-seven years in Upper Montclair, New Jersey. They have three children, seven grandchildren plus two by marriage, and one great grandchild, "all talented and brilliant, of course."

> "LAUGHTER AND A GOOD NIGHT'S SLEEP
> ARE THE TWO BEST CURES."
> *Irish Proverb*

MARGUERITE LOUCKS DYE has been writing for years, but only recently concentrating on humorous poetry, much of it "poking good-natured fun at us Seniors."

She has been a travel agent since 1970 as the result of the couple's love of traveling the globe. They like celebrating anniversaries on a cruise – #57 in February, 1996 – perhaps because they were married in a 37 degree below zero South Dakota Blizzard.

They spend winters on FLORIDA'S Gulf Coast, and summers in the Green Mountains of VERMONT, "in the Ski House we built with our own bare, calloused hands, – my husband's dream and my nightmare for years. (He is vindicated now that it has become a real house with running water – whether it rains or not; electricity – instead of a Coleman two-burner camp stove; indoor plumbing – instead of an outhouse; and walls of glass - - instead of a tent or basement.)"

She loves entertaining, having fun and making people laugh. She hopes her poems will offer readers A SMILE, A CHUCKLE, OR A LOUD GUFFAW.

Her motto is: LAUGH AND LIVE LONGER!

Dear Reader:

> *I hope that these poems will bring you a smile, a chuckle or a loud guffaw, and will brighten your life for a little while.*
>
> *Marguerite Loucks Dye*

- INDEX OF POEMS -

A SMILE
A CHUCKLE
OR
A LOUD
GUFFAW

WHAT DAY IS TODAY?

At breakfast a woman asked her husband
"Do you know what day this is, my dear?"
He squirmed and said, "Of course I do.
You don't think I'd forget such a date this year?"

He seldom remembered their anniversary
And immediately knew "I've done it again!"
When he went to his office he ordered red roses
To be sent to their home – bought chocolates, and then

He went to the jeweler – selected a brooch
Next he phoned her, "Please meet me for dinner tonight."
He ordered champagne at their favorite restaurant.
They toasted each other in warm candlelight.

She was ecstatic and thrilled to her toes –
Flowers, chocolates, jewelry – happy wife.
After champagne and dinner she sighed and then said,
"Today's the best Ground Hog Day of my life!"

NOT READY

I've heard people talk about getting their house
"In dying order" – sparkling and neat.
If I don't die 'til my house is THAT clean,
I expect to live a LONG TIME, my sweet.

THE NORTH-SOUTH ANNUAL TREK
OF SOME SENIORS

We spend our winters on a canal
With my husband's yacht outside the door –
A fourteen foot runabout that runs about half time,
And golf, beach and fun awaiting, and more.

Our cool Vermont summers are happily spent
In the Ski House we built with our bare, calloused hands.
We probably never will use the word "finished"
So we still slave and labor to beat the band.

"I wonder how long we can keep this up?"
I said to my husband who was putting some gear
On top of our wagon – loaded to the gills –
"This packing's a big pain, year after year."

Spending half our time in Florida Paradise
And half in Vermont which we love as well,
We really do have the best of both worlds,
But getting from "here to there" is HELL!

I really don't know why, because we buy
Duplicates of things we won't need to squeeze in.
But for some unknown reason, by the time the car's loaded
There's not even room for a bobby pin.

My husband blames me – "It's your dresses and shoes."
And I must admit, I do take a lot.
But for SIX months I need both work and dress clothes,
And on top of all that – for cold weather and hot.

I need rain gear and jackets and sweaters because
It is COLD in Vermont in the early morn.
But some days are hot in the afternoon.
I leave in Vermont the tattered and torn

Cont. on next page.

It's often snowing when we depart
The Frozen North so I need to wear boots.
Then I have to remember to pack them again
Though it's hot, and I hate to add more to the loot.

I surely can see why friends *finally* decide
To sell their Northern vacation home
And plan to spend summers in Florida
With visits to children, and some time to roam.

I suppose we'll succumb to it too one day
'Cuz the packing and loading gets harder each year.
But as long as we both can just hang in there
We'll continue the trek – and TRY for less gear.

SUDDEN MAKEOVER

I need a new gown. I must go to town,
And while I am there, I'll see to my hair.
I should get it cut – at least a new style
'Cuz soon I'll see friends I have missed for a while.

I must get a facial and eyebrows plucked,
A manicure and girdle to keep my waist tucked.
I'll buy sexy shoes with heels quite high
And a stole that will promise to catch every eye.

Better get my teeth whitened. I may have a date.
I've got to lose weight. I'm sorry I ate!
"Why are you torturing yourself? Please speak."
"I'm going to my High School reunion next week!"

FIFTY YEARS OF WEDDED BLISS

"So you have been married for fifty years!
Do you have a secret sublime—
A recipe making a marriage last?"
"Yes, three little words that I say all the time."

"How sweet," the reporter gushed, "Do you tell her
'I love you' in prose or in song?"
"No, the words I repeat every day of my life
Are those SHE wants to hear – 'I was wrong!' "

A MARRIED MAN

"I've a secret. I'm in love with a married man,
And what's more, I have been for years."
"I'm shocked at you. Aren't you ashamed of yourself?"
"No I'm not 'cuz he's married to ME, my dear."

ˌTY OLD GUY

randfather always salted his food
re he even tasted it.
ˌhook the shaker vigorously
ˌ scorned those who used just a little bit.

ˌ had a pat answer for any who'd say,
 ˏou shouldn't use so much salt!" He'd spat,
"ˌon't tell _me_ not to use so much salt!
I buried three doctors who told me that."

NIFTY FREEBIE GIFTIES

I don't think I've ever been jealous
But I did come close at times
'Cuz my high school friends had dads who brought home
Samples from all their lines.

One salesman father gave my friend
Three brand new pairs of shoes.
A candy store owner gave another
Boxes of chocolates and caramel chews.

One papa sold books, and so he took home
Stacks of gems for my friend to read.
Another pop owned a bicycle shop
And he gave my friend a velocipede.

But woe was I! My dear old guy
Was a lawyer, though really nice –
Instead of shoes, candy, books and toys
All I got was free advice.

SPRING IS SPRUNG

It's hard to improve on my favorite poem
Of Springtime.   The Brooklyn Chant –
"Spring is sprung. The grass is riz.
I wondah where the posies is.

They say the boids is on the wing.
Now ain't that absoid?
'Cuz peoples know it just can't be. - -
The wings is on da boid."

The "Virtues of Spring" are extolled by poets.
The "Awakening of Spirit" in both young and old.
They write of "Rebirth of the Body and Soul"—
"The Beginnings of Life" in the midst of the cold.

BUT – if you live in the North, while buds shoot forth
Spring means hard work. Aching muscles will shout.
Storm windows first come off, then screens must go on
After windows are washed both inside and out.

The buds may be sprouting, but that leaves some pouting
'Cuz now one must fertilize – dig up anew.
The whole yard needs raking, the bedding needs shaking.
Oh where to begin – there is so much to do!

The garden needs tilling, then raking and smoothing
Preparing for seeds that are ready to plant.
Then they all need water. Tomatoes need stakes.
The chores are on-going. Some just rave and rant.

Furniture must leave the garage for the porch,
Be scraped and then painted – the cushions spruced up.
The hammock needs dusting and hung on strong hooks
All set for relaxing – both feet can go up.

Then all window boxes must be filled with flowers
And perhaps they need scraping and painting, too.
A trip to the nursery – decisions galore –
For top soil, peat moss, a new plant or two.

Cont. next page

Both basement and garage need old fashioned cleaning.
Remember when we would beat rugs on the line?
And draperies were aired, then stored for the summer
And replaced by some sheer ones? Then all could be fine.

We know that the birds are migrating now
And the buds are all bursting anew.
The bleak, barren landscape will soon come to life
And the brown grass will turn to a lovely green hue.

In South Dakota Spring means rain
And often snow for many hours.
Spirits, though damp, are kept up high, with
"April showers will bring May flowers."

In Vermont Spring means MUD. It's true as can be.
Getting stuck's not a matter of "If" , but "When."
So being towed out is just par for the course.
Vermonters take mud in their stride. Then they win.

But Springtime in Florida is different 'cuz Seniors
Can enjoy all the buds shooting forth.
Most live in a condo, play tennis and golf.
They left cares and their chores way back up in the North.

So let Spring be sprung. There's no work to be done.
We can go for a swim in the Bay today –
Or a walk on the beach – take a cruise in a boat.
In our dotage, though Spring, we can play.

A LITTLE YOLK

During the depression my father, a lawyer,
Was paid fairly often with food –
Produce like apples, potatoes and corn,
And chicken, both uncooked or stewed.

A farmer was chuckling one day when he came
And my mother said, "Olaf, what's funny?"
He said he had just been next door to deliver.
His loud laughter made his nose runny.

The neighbor had asked, "What's the price of your eggs?
I'm making an angel food cake for my cousin."
"The large ones are forty, the cracked, twenty-five."
Then she'd smiled and said, "Crack me a dozen."

A WEIGHTY PROBLEM

Each decade I seem to have gained a few pounds.
The inches add up over years.
I tug and I pull, but can't zip to the flap.
Do you think I could call this "A Generation Gap?"

(Shades of Greta Garbo)
I VANT TO BE ALONE

Said a mother of seven so mired and tired,
"This is one of my most fervent wishes –
'I Vant Time Alone NOW' ", then she figured out how –
She simply began washing dishes.

MOTHER'S VERY OWN DAY

After a big family Mother's Day Dinner
Mom started to scrub lots of Corning.
Said the children, "It's YOUR day.
              You shouldn't wash dishes!
Just RINSE, and do them in the morning."

DON'T CALL ME A MELON!

"I wish you'd stop calling me a melon!"
A man grumbled to his wife as he donned his hat.
"I've never called you a melon, dear."
"Well, it's 'Honey-dew this and honey-dew that!' "

PATIENT I'M NOT

Lately I've run very short
Of patience, it's really true.
I hate to wait for anyone
When I have things to do.

So now I have composed a prayer
That I say every day.
"Lord grant me please more patience –
And give it to me right away."

THOUGHT PROVOKING

There's something amiss
Kept quiet as a mouse –
We paid more for our new car
Than for our old house.

NAMING THE BABY

I was born at the time of World War I.
My Mom thought my Dad was daft
'Cuz he wanted to name me "Weather-strip"
Since I kept him out of the draft.

THE DISAPPEARING ACT

We Seniors are always losing things.
Perhaps "misplacing" is a kinder word.
It's "Now you have it – now you don't."
It's gone, and we feel like a nerd.

Coin purse, name tags, car keys –
Dark glasses and even toast –
But of all the things I've lost this year
I miss my mind the most.

LAZYBONES

"You're the laziest man I've ever met,
So why do they call you a go-getter?"
" 'Cuz after my wife works a nine hour day
I leave my soft chair and go get her."

HOW COULD YOU? or IT NEVER FAILS!

I remember when I was a bride long ago
And would cook something special – a neat treat
with a punch - -
"Guess what! I've made Maine lobster thermidor
with shrimp!"
"That's just what I had for lunch with the bunch."

A VERY LONG, REALLY BAD SERMON

A long-winded preacher was going on and on.
The members were squirming and fit to be tied.
At long last a brave soul got up to walk out
The preacher was miffed at his rudeness, so pried:

"Why are you leaving and where are you going?"
"To get me a haircut," replied angry Ben.
"Why did you not get a haircut before?"
"Because, I didn't need one then."

HOW GOOD WAS THAT SERMON?
(Our minister told this story at a Religious Literature
Seminar)

"THAT was a damn good sermon you gave!"
The minister bristled and hastily said,
"Don't use that language in a Holy Place!"
He was so upset his face was red.

"No kidding! It was the best damn one that I've ever heard!"
This time the minister fumed and turned gray.
"It was so damn good I gave a $100.00 bill."
The minister gulped, "The hell, you say."

HAPPY EIGHTIETH BIRTHDAY!

So you are celebrating your 80th birthday!
Are you not the LUCKY ONE?
You've lived through many ups and downs
But today is YOUR DAY in the sun.

You've managed to rise above good times and bad.
You never gave up. You kept on the run.
You weren't even slowed down by wind, ice or hail.
So today is YOUR DAY in the sun.

You've lived a fine life – have many good friends –
A family that loves you and memories of fun.
You've weathered the storms of rain, sleet and snow,
Now today is YOUR DAY in the sun.

We wish you a glorious and memorable birthday
With many to follow in good health. You've won!
May all your breezes be gentle and kind.
Enjoy to the hilt YOUR DAY in the sun!

QUOTABLE QUOTE

It made me smile to hear a quote
Of an elder citizen so deft,
"I started out with nuthin' and
I still have some of it left."

ONE WAY TO BEAT THE ODDS

"What can I do? I'm getting so old.
My wrinkles have wrinkles all over my face.
Please give me advice. I use packs of ice
But they are no help – not one little trace."

"My only suggestion for you is to look
For a husband like mine. It's simple. You see,
I married a fine anthropologist, so
The older I get, the better he likes me."

STAYING FIT

Some older men were comparing notes
On what great shape they were in.
One man said, "I jog four miles a day
And that's what keeps me trim and thin."

Another said, "I keep ship-shape
By playing lots of golf and tennis."
One old gent said, "It's bowling for me."
"Shuffleboard and horseshoes," said a man named Dennis.

"I can do the same number of push-ups
I did when I was twenty-one."
They oohed and aahed then asked, "How many?"
He squirmed, then finally admitted, "None."

SOMETIME SOON

One of these days I'm going to lose weight,
Cut down on calories, and I'll exercise.
I'll lower my fat and cholesterol
Watch salt intake and cut out fries.

One of these days I'll make up a schedule
Of things to do to keep me healthy.
I'm going to walk – so far it's just "talk."
I'll save calories and money 'til I get wealthy.

One of these days I'll get more sleep.
Stop burning the candle at both of the ends.
I'll learn to say , "No." I'll slow down – not go
Every minute of my waking hours. Amen.

One of these days I'll learn to relax.
I'll read all the books I've been saving to savor.
The recipes, articles I've clipped will get filed –
All letters answered, cook from scratch for more flavor.

One of these days I'll turn over a new leaf
No more type 'A' for me. (I'll bet!)
I'll be so laid back you won't recognize me –
One of these days – but not yet.

DIVORCE RESULTS

"I hate my wife for what she did!
She made me a millionaire!"
"Are you crazy? How could you hate her for THAT?"
"'Cuz I used to be a billionaire."

CHANDELIER IN THE FOYER

The church entrance hall was as dark as could be.
This bothered parishioners for many long years.
From time to time this brought heated discussions,
But the hall remained dark, in spite of some tears.

One day an old Elder did fall in the hall.
He was angry and shouted, "We need a chandelier!
Here's a written request. Take it up at your meeting
And PLEASE don't put THIS off again 'til next year."

When the session was over the elder appeared.
"Did you vote to install a new chandelier
In our front hall? You KNOW how badly we need it!"
"Naw, we did not," for all to hear.

"In the first place the secretary couldn't spell it.
And none of the committee could pronounce it at all.
And most of us thought when we did have the money
We really should put up a light in the hall."

SOMETHING TO THINK ABOUT

"When I wake up," said a vigorous elder
"I decide between being <u>The Statue or The Bird</u>.
But IF I have <u>three</u> statue days in a row
I must do something FAST, or I'll end up a nerd."

MAGIC IN THE SKY

A week ago we saw the COMET
HYAKUTAKI. What a thrill!
I thought I'd jump right out of my skin
I was so excited. I couldn't stand still.

First we found the Big Dipper in the North
And below it a few bright stars,
Then further under, a blurry light
Like the Milky Way, but smaller by far.

This COMET was only recently discovered
—Won't re-appear for countless years.
What a joy to find it, and actually see it.
The sight of the night was filled with cheers.

We saw the ECLIPSE OF THE MOON last night
With our binoculars, -- also without.
The large orange ball slowly disappeared
While clouds kept passing in and out.

Then, little by little, a crescent-white-light
At the bottom grew larger and larger, and then
There was so much light it hurt eyes with binoculars –
At last, a bright, full moon again.

In about 3000 years there'll be another.
(Don't ask how astronomers know they are right.)
But we couldn't wait, so how lucky we are that
We saw the ECLIPSE OF THE MOON last night.

      So much excitement! I can hardly take it.
      If there's any more soon, I'll just have to fake it.

SENIORS AT PLAY
(BRIDGE, ANYONE?)

If you want a good laugh, watch us Seniors at play.
It's a riot to look or to listen.
We ask, "Who dealt this?" or "Whose lead is it now?"
We are trying so hard our brows glisten.

We have a good time while we gossip and bid,
It bothers some not they don't make it.
We blame it on cards that were dealt us (too low)
We'll just try again, or we'll fake it.

"I hope you don't mind that we're going to go down,
But I thought that perhaps we might make it,"
Is just one excuse for a bidding abuse.
We have many, but know how to take it.

"I thought we could keep them from making a rubber.
They have sixty on toward a game,"
Is another thing heard from the voice of a nerd
Who's an otherwise smart and bright dame.

You're likely to hear the same phrases so near
If you walk from one table to another.
"Breast your cards," "It's your lead," "No, I dealt them last time,"
"Well, we almost made it." Oh, Brother!

We all have one trouble is common.
A nuisance, a bore we regret.
From May to December, we cannot remember.
Our common bond is "We Forget."

"Would you <u>review</u> the bidding once more for me please?"
Is a question that's heard fairly often.
But hearing it twice, leads to hearing it thrice.
Some think we should be in a coffin.

Cont. on next page

We each have infirmities – one kind or another.
We could all give up bridge in disgust –
But to see how we help one another at play
is heart warming to each one of us.

Some can't hear, some can't see, some can't hold the cards,
And others can't reach to the dummy.
But, by George, we are trying. It's better than dying,
So the on-lookers better keep mummy.

If a person is deaf, we use signals to bid.
If a heart then we tap on our heart.
For a diamond we point to our left finger's ring
To denote what we're trying to impart.

We pound on our arm if we mean to bid clubs.
Pretending to dig is for spades.
Kibitzers must think that we've all gone berserk
When they spy us each doing our charades.

The cataract victims need bold and large print.
These decks are salvation for many.
A few claim they can't use such big cards at all –
"Too disturbing!" They're not having any.

Some can't hold all cards in their hand at one time
But they manage to grip a round "holder"
That grasps all the cards in a circular fan
And makes those with arthritis be bolder.

When someone is obviously struggling to bid
And some time has elapsed. They're in pain.
There's always a kinder and gentler reminder,
"Remember, it's only a game."

"Three passes to you," can cause one to squirm
And count honors, and count them again.
"I would bid if I could, but I think that I should
Just say 'Pass' with my weak count of ten."

Cont. on next page

31.

We never get teary, though often we're weary
Of runs of a one-Jack-high hand.
But hope springs eternal as equinox vernal,
So it's bridge for a stout-hardy band.

"We'll have to be cautious. We're vulnerable now."
Is the warning we give to each other.
"I had one hundred honors so I lost my head." –
One excuse, for going down, to another.

"It soon will be over and we'll be in clover
Unless our opponents will double."
"In that case I'll pass," said one undaunted lass,
"Or we'll find ourselves deeper in trouble."

"It's the last hand today, so let's shuffle and play
Though they've set us three times in a row.
But I have a good hand, so I'm bidding 'Demand'.
We may go *down* in a glorious glow."

When St. Peter calls us to his Pearly Gates,
There's a question that we will set forth.
It's "Why did you call? I was having a ball!"
And he'll answer, "I needed a fourth."

HELPFUL HARRY

A just-married elderly couple checked in
To a lavish hotel their first night.
The bridegroom went into the bathroom and stayed
While the bride primped in bed, feeling high as a kite.

When her husband emerged from the bathroom at last
"Are you alright, my dear?" she did coo.
"I did all my chores, then brushed my teeth,
And while I was at it, I brushed yours, too."

HAPPY BIRTHDAY!

A man was greeting his friend who turned eighty.
"You really don't age. You still look fine!
How does it feel to be eighty?" he asked.
"I don't feel a day over seventy-nine."

I FORGET

Seniors were discussing their memory problems.
One man stood up and proclaimed in a fit,
"I've done it all, seen it all, and I've heard it all, too,
But I just can't remember one dang bit of it!"

NOW MY UMBRELLA IS SAFE

The men in my life used to borrow my umbrella
When theirs were nowhere to be found.
I tried many things, besides hiding it,
But often when needed, it was no place around.

I finally dreamed up a nifty idea.
I bought an umbrella – PINK with a RUFFLE!
No matter the weather, they leave it alone,
So the problem was solved, without a scuffle.

CRAZY ENDINGS

In South Dakota when I was young,
We dreamed up endings for ads as we played –
"They laughed when I sat down at the piano, - -
BUT THEY CRIED REAL TEARS WHEN I PLAYED."

YOU WANT TO SIT WHERE?

A usher pointed out a couple he'd seated.
"I know they are new to our church," he did tease,
"'Cuz when I asked where they'd prefer to sit,
They answered, 'In non-smoking, please.' "

FLORIDA'S SENSATIONAL SENIORS

Some Florida elders are chipper and lively.
They're on the go both day and night.
Instead of a rocker they're out playing soccer,
And the gals – at the Spa, wearing tights.

The children up north think their elderly parents
Have retired to lie in the sun.
What they don't know won't hurt them
      (No need to alert them.)
They're both on the run having fun.

Said one man who was tired because he retired
"This merry-go-round's not for me.
I'll get me a job so my sleep I won't rob,
And besides, I'll have my weekends free."

HORRIBLE HORS D'OEUVRES

A husband whispered to his wife
"These snacks are AWFUL they've served with the beer!"
"You silly! No wonder you don't like the taste.
You're eating the pot-pourri, my dear."

A DIFFERENT INTERPRETATION

A doctor was scolding a lazy patient
Who hated exercise – "It makes me delirious."
The doctor decided to hold no punches –
"Listen to me, Sam! This is serious!

I want you to play <u>eighteen holes</u> every day
Beginning today, until Hanukkah."
So Sam went to a store that he'd been to before
And bought for himself a harmonica.

OPTIONS

Said a broker who tried to sell stocks
To a ninety year old named Marannas,
"Ten year bonds will make money."
 She said, "Listen, Sonny,
I don't even buy green bananas!"

BURNING BACON or WHEN DO WE EAT?

"What time is breakfast?" My husband asked.
"I can't be late for golf."
"Breakfast will be ready," I said,
"When the smoke alarm goes off."

SQUEAKING HEARING AIDS

It's hard to live within an income,
But even harder to live without it.
The same is true of a hearing aid.
I can hardly hear with it, but can't hear without it.

The constant squealing is driving me crazy –
And squawking and making such loud weird noises –
The clatter of dishes, air conditioning, coughs, sneezes –
It magnifies ALL but human voices.

America has progressed to a fare-thee-well.
They can search under water and walk on the moon.
I can only hope that in my lifetime
They'll develop a decent hearing aid SOON.

ON DEAFNESS

Being hard of hearing is
Frustrating! Such a bore!
The only good thing about it is - -
I can't hear my husband snore.

A THANKSGIVING PRAYER FROM AN OLDIE

Thank you, God, for the gift of LAUGHTER,
For loud guffaws, chuckles and smiles.
I'm grateful I have a funny-bone
That goes off often – makes life worthwhile.

I thank you for ENTHUSIASM.
It helps to bring excitement each day.
I'm glad I find joy in simple things –
Sunsets on the Bay and children at play.

I'm blessed with GOOD HEALTH and HIGH ENERGY
So I can run both night and day,
But I claim I'm NOT a workaholic
'Cuz I'm all for fun, and love to play.

I thank you for my many FRIENDS.
They color my life such beautiful hues.
Their acts of kindness and many calls –
Their letters and hugs keep away the blues.

You gave me a special FAMILY –
The very best in the world, I know.
My husband, children, grandchildren and great
Are absolute tops. They keep me aglow.

We've heard, "Love makes the world go 'round,"
So most of all I give thanks for LOVE –
My love for you, my family and friends –
I know it's sent from heaven above.

Amen

GAINING GRADUALLY

"What would you like for dessert tonight?"
I asked my husband who's lean.
"Why not make your chocolate cake
That's dripping with fudge and whipped cream?"

That chocolate cake is calorie high
And far from cholesterol free,
But at our age, who cares anyway?
We can diet tomorrow at three.

We're chocoholic freaks for sure
Devouring cookies, brownies and cake.
My husband is thin, but now I waddle.
I'm gaining because I bake.

Marguerite's Ooh-la-la Hot Fudge Sauce
Is my undoing, I fear,
But family and friends often ask for it,
So, there's more of me to love each year.

MY FAVORITE RECIPE

Some women were trading recipes.
"Mine's the best MEATLOAF one about.
I only have to mention it
And my husband says, '*Let's eat out.*' "

HOW DO I GET FROM HERE TO THERE?

My husband and I seem to drive a lot
So we often need to ask directions.
Some of the answers that we've been given
Have made us laugh, but need correction.

In Maine we looked for a very small town.
We saw an old codger – thought "This is a cinch."
"Which way is the town of Holly, please?"
"Doncha move a gol dern inch."

In Puerto Rico my husband asked
Directions getting gas from a man with a flair.
Our friend said, "I think we're really in trouble.
He's pointing his arm straight up in the air."

One of my favorites occurred in Vermont.
We asked a young boy on a bike by a tree,
"How do you get to Rutland from here?"
He said, "My mother always drives me."

The most common thing that people do
When giving directions – some not so deft,
Is saying "Turn RIGHT when you get to the fork,"
But with their hand they are pointing LEFT.

Remember this story? A violinist asked a policeman,
"How do you get to Carnegie Hall?"
The policeman, a musician himself, thought then said,
"Practice, practice, practice! That's all."

We all remember the story so old
About a drunk giving help by ear.
He thought, changed his mind, thought again, then said,
"You know what? It's true! You can't get there from here!"

A PAPER SAVER

I can't remember back far enough
To a time I didn't save paper.
Unwrapping a gift is wonderful fun,
Both the present and paper I savor.

I fold gift-wrapping carefully
So I can use it again.
I do the same with ribbons and bows.
Then I iron both in the den.

My family has teased me over the years.
They think I am cheap, one hundred percent.
Now I say, "I'm environmentally correct."
And fold, save and iron to my heart's content.

IT'S TIME NOW

The string beans are purple. Jolly Giant is red.
I stare as a chef performs his salad-mixing.
Cucumbers are pink, the radishes blue –
It's time to admit that the TV needs fixing.

HOW DO YOU GET YOUR HIGHS?

It's fun for me to hear people tell
How they get they're HIGHS in life.
They run the gamut from here to there
To relieve both tension and strife.

It doesn't take much to give me a HIGH.
A black lab or yellow with tail wagging,
Or seeing a baby so smiling and sweet,
Or a beautiful sunset with a little light lagging.

One man said, "For me, it's a Hole-in-One."
Said another, "When I bowl two thirty plus."
Said a gal to a pal, "When I flirt at a bar."
And "In tennis a GAME when friends make a fuss."

Flea markets are tops for many people.
Getting a bargain gives us a big rush.
The low prices we paid for our "find" makes us brag
And show off our prize 'til friends wish we would hush.

Some gals are whizzes at sewing.
They knit beautiful sweaters – can also crochet.
They design fancy T-Shirts with sequins and jewels.
Display of their talents makes quite an array.

"I get a HIGH going fast in my boat,"
Said a man, "Barely skimming the water's a thrill."
"Carving a figure from a piece of wood
Is relaxing. It saves my taking a pill."

The men in my life get a thrill when they fish
If a fighter gets hooked on their line.
And they like many sports, such as football and hockey –
To play it or watch it suits them just fine.

At Fairs I LOVE rides – the wilder the better!
(Some people grow up and others do not.)
And rhythmical music gets under my skin.
I cannot stand still when the music is hot.

Cont. on next page

42.

No matter how bushed, I could dance all night.
The music thrills me to my toes.
I like to eat, but I'd rather dance.
While I twirl and swirl I forget any woes.

I love to wander and travel the globe.
Sight-seeing is high on my list of HIGHS.
Foreign countries with sights, sounds and scents so strange
Thrill me to the core and provide happy sighs.

Getting letters from family and friends gives a boost
To my morale in a very big way.
Grandchildren and children who write and send photos
Offer oldies more joy than we ever can say.

It's exciting for me to sort my cards
For a bridge game. There's always such HOPE.
But when it's jack high, I hear Dogers cry,
"Wait 'til next year!" Then I mope.

I feel good each time that my family
Tells me I've baked a scrumptious cake.
And I love it when friends really laugh at my jokes
Or stories I tell for fun's sake.

Hearing audiences laugh makes me feel so great
When I read my poems to groups large or small.
Another HIGH – seeing my work in print - -
That just might be the best HIGH of all.

GENEALOGY AT NINE

My grandson, Danny, makes me laugh.
He's funny, punny and witty.
We often do crazy things together
And end up writing a silly ditty.

I said, "Where do you get your good sense of humor?"
"I can't help it, Gammy. It's in my genes."
Then he thrust his hand is his dungaree pocket –
"Also in my jeans are a flashlight and beans."

A GRANDMOTHER'S URGENT REQUEST

A grandmother attending her grandson's wedding
Was shocked at how loud the band was playing.
She said, "It's so loud it's coming through my veins!
Can't take another minute. My body is aching."

She mustered up courage to speak to the leader.
Yelling, on tip toes, she became a shouter:
"Can't you DO SOMETHING about the MUSIC?"
"Sorry, Lady. I can't get it any louder!"

LIKE DEAR OLD DAD

On his fiftieth birthday he looked in the mirror
And saw a strong likeness to his father.
Later that day he answered someone –
"That's just what Dad would have said, '*Why bother?*' "

That evening he happily told his mother
He thought he was getting to be like his dad.
He laughed when his mother just smiled and said,
"Now there's a scary thought to be had."

EXERCISING WITH GRANDMA

A Grandma had scolded a naughty grandchild
Who was watching her doing some knee bends.
She suggested he try doing them with her that day
So they did them together, just to make amends.

He tried hard to copy but was so displeased.
She said, "You are bending like I am. It's true."
He said, "No, Gram, I'm *not*. I'm trying so hard
But I can't make that cracking sound like you can do."

WHERE OH WHERE ARE GRANDMA AND GRANDPA?

Grandma's line dancing and NOT making cookies,
She's golfing or playing some bridge.
She's out having fun or she's soaking up sun,
But she's NOT making fudge for the fridge.

Her scrubbing and cleaning and baking and mending
Have gone by the board with the blues.
When asked why she now is avoiding it all
She just shrugs and says, "I've paid my dues."

That she's not in the kitchen and cooking up cakes
Is a puzzle, and some think it strange.
She could be out gambling, or dancing a square,
But you won't find her home on the range.

She's making up time that she lost in her prime,
For the years she stood over the sink.
The housedress is gone with the gray hair, now blonde,
She's off in her boots and her mink.

She swims in her pool before breakfast,
Then jogs on the beach for a mile.
When she loses a pound – finds she's not so round,
She's delighted. That makes grandma smile.

She goes to the spa several mornings,
Joins friends for some wine and a quiche,
Then they all have a ball shopping down at the Mall
Before sunning themselves on the beach.

She bowls with her team every Tuesday,
Has board meetings monthly at church.
She sings in Chorale – this is one busy gal –
Never seems to be left in the lurch

Cont. on next page

The children all wonder what happened
To the homebody-mother they knew.
She used to bake brownies and pies every week –
Now she shuns sweets and diets on cue.

The offspring each groan, and moan when they phone,
In fact, they all get in a tizzy.
"You NEVER are home! Where oh where do you roam?
It rings and it rings, or it's busy!"

What's happening to Grandpa while Grandma
Is off "Doing her thing" to the hilt?
He's out on his own, or he's still on the phone,
And HIS pace makes a lesser man wilt.

Grandpa is golfing or hiking or fishing,
Or working on trailer or boat.
He watches the market on TV
Trying to keep their finances afloat.

He studies his dear Wall Street Journal,
Though he buys high and often sells low.
But "Someday" he'll say, "I've hit pay dirt today!"
And they'll celebrate. "Yippee I-O!

One chore that does rile is going through the pile
And trying to keep up with the mail.
Does his own income tax, so he cannot relax
Though he'd rather be going for a sail.

Auctions, flea markets, and local yard sales
Are haunts that he likes to attend.
Grandpa has a collection of cast iron rejections –
His fry pans are laid end to end.

Cont. on next page

Grandpa calls the golf club to get tee time.
He gets up before dawn to phone,
Then notifies buddies to tell them the hour
And whose riding a cart all alone.

When Grandma suggests "Let's eat out,"
Grandpa answers her fast with a smile,
"Should we eat in the front yard or back yard?"
Which makes Grandma miffed at his guile.

The Early Bird Special's a big thing
For Seniors to save on their meals.
They leave bright and early to get there on time
And save money to kick up their heels.

They're living their life in the fast lane still.
They've heard, "If you rest you will rust."
Every hour of the day they're at work or at play.
Their motto is, "Do it or bust!"

At the drop of a hat they will travel
By plane or by ship or by car
To a far-away place at a really fast pace.
They climb hills to sight-see from afar.

They've heard you must "Use it or lose it"
To stay healthy and keep in the pink.
So they move night and day, entertain, dance and play,
And at night pass out "quick as a wink."

Up North they both called it "A Rat Race"
Of duties piled high as a mound.
But since they retired and they're not so mired
They call it "A Merry-Go-Round."

When Grandma and Grandpa retired, they moved
To Florida, far from the cold.
They're active, healthy and happy as clams.
Now THAT is the way to grow old!

WHAT HAPPENED WHEN I WASN'T LOOKING?
or
A SENIOR CITIZEN'S LAMENT

In my youth I could laugh at the so-silly words
"My get up and go has got up and went."
But I'm not laughing now! It's funny no more.
My whole body says the last cent has been spent.

It's a mystery to me. I just cannot see
Why I can't "Do it all" like I did.
Must I cry on your shoulder because I am older?
But the truth – I've slowed even my id.

When I wasn't looking my energy went.
It's for certain. There's something amiss.
I used to hip-hop, now I'm three gears from stop.
It's disgusting to slow down like this.

I need high octane liquids like very strong coffee
To help me get moving each day.
But my zip's zapped by noon, which is really too soon,
And by night time I'm too bushed to play.

What happened to all of that high energy
That I used to have? What a surprise!
I had bounce to the ounce. I was ready to pounce,
And was rarin' to go at sunrise.

It wasn't so long ago I could continue
To work and exhaust those around me – but
Now my anchor is draggin' and everything's saggin'.
Can I blame it on old age, or what?

My children and grandchildren said, "Please slow down!
It's too hard to keep up with your pace."
But I couldn't resist going both day and night,
And I ran like I was in a race.

Cont. on next page

But now I am shuffling one foot, then the other
And feel really far from tip-top.
Frustration is heading the list of my feelings –
It's no fun to be too pooped to pop.

I've decided my problem is two-fold in nature.
It's *sleep deprivation* and *sheer dehydration*.
I feel better with this diagnosis. Now what
Will decide my well-being? Just determination.

I'll cure myself soon of this rotten malaise.
I'll go to bed early and drink lots of water.
Think – "Get me more sleep!" and "Push lots of liquids!"
And soon I should shape up again like I oughter.

My new regime's working! I'm better already!
If I follow it closely it should be a snap.
I can't tell you more now because I must go
And drink lots of water and then take a nap.
                Z Z Z Z Z Z Z Z Z Z Z Z Z Z

ALERT! HOUSE GUESTS ARE COMING!

HELP! House guests are coming. This place is a mess!
What should I do first? I can't even guess.

My husband has papers from here to there.
Wherever I look, they are everywhere.

The guest room is littered with files galore –
The bed, table, chairs – and even the floor.

It wasn't a chore when our house was big –
If things piled up and we lived like a pig.

We could open a door, pile things on the floor
To our heart's content, and then close the door,

But our house is small now. There's nowhere to hide,
And no extra drawer to stuff something inside.

Cont. on next page

He won't let me touch things. He thinks he'll lose track
Of important papers he's carefully stacked.

I think I'm going crazy. I can't find the bed.
I've got to change sheets, but it's cluttered instead.

I've made my hot fudge sauce and chocolate cake,
And aspic. The brownies are ready to bake.

I've dusted and vacuumed and hidden away
A pile of loose items that got in my way,

But the guest room's not ready! If it will be, can't tell.
They're coming tomorrow! I'm nervous as h---.

He's SO relaxed but I'm in a tizzy.
The guest room's a shambles. Why isn't he busy?

Instead of sorting and tossing papers
He's reading his Journal and doing other capers.

We need a small miracle to be ready on time.
He's doing his tax now, I'll bet you a dime.

My stress is high-level. It's way off the chart.
My track shoes are greased and I'm ready to dart.

If a miracle happens, as miracles do,
Don't look under beds, whatever you do!

HOIDY-TOIDY

A doctor sent an arrogant lady
To a lab for tests – some blood work, too.
When the Grande-Dame saw the vile of blood –
"This CAHN'T be MINE! My blood is BLUE!"

IS SHE OR IS SHE NOT A BACK SEAT DRIVER?

A man was complaining to his friend
That his wife was a back seat driver.
"Is your wife one too? I'd like to know.
Most likely! I'll bet you a fiver."

"Whether my wife is a back seat driver
Is not for me to say.
But from Vermont to Florida I drove half way
And my wife drove all the way."

THE MAYBE OR MAYBE NOT YACHT

Our grandchildren love to be given a ride
On what I call "Grandpapa's Yacht."
It's a fourteen foot run-about that runs about half time,
And gets towed back more often than not.

Our daughter loves going for a ride in the boat.
She says, "For excitement Pop does have the knack.
You meet such nice people when you go with him
'Cuz you never know who'll tow you back."

I'M GLAD I'M HERE INSTEAD OF THERE

The palm trees are swaying. The sea breeze is blowing.
Above is a cloudless blue sky.
I turn on my TV and soon I do see
Snow, high as an elephant's eye.

I watch people scraping their icy windshields,
Wearing wool scarves covering their mouth.
A fierce storm in the North is now raging forth,
But I'm snug as a bug in a rug in the South.

I view cars that have landed in six foot snowbanks,
And trucks that have slid off the road.
The plows are all out. I can hear people shout,
But I'm warm down here in my abode.

I see vehicles lurching and slipping and sliding
On icy and treacherous roads.
The temperature's dropped. Most traffic has stopped.
Sand trucks are out spreading their loads.

With horror I watch as twelve cars rear-end.
In the den I see roads slick with ice.
The bedroom TV shows a pile-up of trucks.
I watch more in the kitchen while cooking fried rice.

I see people sledding and some making snowmen.
It's fun. They're not cold, so they say.
But I'd rather build sand castles down on the beach
Or just go for a swim in the bay.

I've decided that "cold" is for young people now,
And "cozy and warm" for the old.
You can have all the snow, and the sleet and the ice –
At my age, on the South I am sold.

I can't leave the TV alone for a minute.
I watch people shovel and sneeze as they freeze.
My blood has thinned out, so the cold makes me pout –
In my dotage I LOVE SNOW ON TV's.

THE BIGGIE LETDOWN

Says latter day philosopher, the great Yogi Berra,
"It's not over 'til it's over." And he is right.
Don't think because Christmas is over, it is
'Cuz it isn't, 'til the tree's down and far out of sight.

The season is gone now and so is the egg nog
And all that is left is one huge sorry mess.
Gift wrapping is littered from here to there –
All sizes of boxes and bows, you can guess.

The presents in piles must be put away.
The lights in the windows have all gotta go.
Outside decorations must sometime come down
In spite of the weather – wind, rain, sleet or snow.

The candles and bells, the angels and santas
Must be carefully wrapped, along with all wreaths.
The tablecloths, napkins, towels, aprons for Christmas
Are laundered and stashed 'til next year under eaves.

Old Scrooge is still mumbling, "Oh, never again!
I'm worn out from parties too often and late.
I've eaten too much of the cookies and candy
And gained weight. Now Christmas I'm starting to hate.

It will be much too soon if I hear one more carol
I'm sick of the Glee Clubs all over the place.
We're probably broke now 'cuz you spent so much
On presents for people at such a fast pace.

Why did we ever pick such a big tree?
Who filled every branch with all of this stuff?
The icicles need to come off one by one?
You gotta be kidding. That's really too tough!

Cont. on next page

Never again are we going all out
On spending, decorating and mailing so much.
No more Christmas letters that tell our life story
To send to our friends just to keep them in touch."

He gripes so each year with fervor and zeal
I think, "This time he means it for sure, poor dear."
But time heals all wounds, and he will recover,
So we'll do it all over again – next year.

HAPPY BIRTHDAY, DEAR WILLARD

You've just turned eighty-three today!
Let's celebrate and not be blue.
You've held your age well and so we can tell
"You don't look a day over eighty-two."

We like your spirit and lust for life
The Vermontclair Palace is your dream come true.
You know it was my worst nightmare for years
But it's livable now so much credit is due you.

You've been a good husband, father and friend
And an active community volunteer for years.
Because of you our world is better!
We offer to you three big, loud cheers.

Happy Birthday, dear Willard. Have fun and be proud.
Rejoice your good health and shed no tears.
We wish you the best! If you keep up your zest
You'll have MANY more glorious and memorable years.

Love,

Marguerite
Your Slave (driver)

August 21, 1996

RECIPE FOR LIVING TO BE ONE HUNDRED

If you'd like to live to be one hundred
Here's how to do it without a tear – –
Just live to be ninety-nine, and then
BE VERY CAREFUL, my dear.

THE UNINVITED GUEST
or
I CAN'T BELIEVE THIS!

We have older friends who claim they're so tired
At night they would rather stay home than to roam.
They LOVE to hear there's a party that night
And they've NOT been invited, so they can stay home.

OLDER AND STIFFER

I laughed when I heard Rodney Dangerfield's joke.
When I told it to others they doubled with glee.
But we're not laughing now that we're older and stiffer.
It's funny no more 'cuz it's true as can be.

Rodney had said, "When I lean down
To pick up something I've dropped mid air,
I look all around just to see if there's anything
Else I should do while I'm down there."

RISE AND SHINE

Getting up in the morning was never a problem.
I'd wake up and bounce out of bed.
Now I open my eyes to the early sunrise
And then sit on the edge of the bed instead.

After a while I grope on the table
For glasses. I need them to see.
Then I find and put in both my hearing aids
So now I can see and hear. Lucky me!

With my cane I shuffle to the bathroom and brush
My teeth that were soaking all night.
I glance in the mirror. Don't like what I see!
Without my toupee I sure look a fright.

Now I wind and wrap my elastic belt
That helps to hold my hernia in place.
Then I put new pads on two bunions and corns
And remember I forgot to wash my face.

It's time to get dressed. Putting socks on is hard.
Then I struggle with shoes, especially the ties.
Now my shirt, then the slacks and the darn belt buckle.
At least I have sworn off wearing neckties.

By George, now I'm dressed so I head for the kitchen
To plug in the coffee and squeeze orange juice.
I'll have bran topped with prunes, two pieces of toast.
I'm set for the day. Now I'll just hang loose!

AT AN AUCTION, SIT ON YOUR HANDS

The Auctioneer's spiel was rapid and loud
Exhorting the merits of ten bales of hay.
"SOLD to the lady in black in the back!"
"Who? Me? I was just waving pipe smoke away."

THE JOYS (?) OF CHRISTMAS EVE
OR
CHAOS IN PARADISE

What happened to the Christmas spirit?
Don't answer that. Can't bear to hear it.
Poor Dad's about to blow a fuse
Assembling toys. Oh, what a ruse!

Kids asleep with all dreams dazzled.
Mom is worn out, tired and frazzled.
She's baked cookies, pies and cakes
Made costumes for the children's sake.

The turkey's set for tomorrow's dinner
For friends and family – a sure winner.
Packages are finally wrapped
But Mom, by now, is really zapped.

The talking doll just will not talk.
The walking duck can't seem to walk.
Dad thinks the Teddy Bear has a smirk.
Even the weatherman's gone berserk.

The trains won't run. The tracks don't fit.
And Dad's about to have a fit.
The missing parts are causing pain
And then he thinks, "No pain, no gain."

"I'll put on carols to help your mood.
You sound like Scrooge. Guess you need food.
Here, have a piece of Christmas candy.
It may help you, Handy Andy.

So he returns to assembling toys
"Can't concentrate. There's too much noise."
Mom asks, "Why must it take an eon?"
"Because the directions are in Korean.

Cont. on next page

And batteries we need are 'C'
And, sad to say, we have only 'D'.
The tools we used were in the car.
The tree's all set – can't find the star."

But all is well on Christmas morn
Though most of the house looks tattered and torn.
The kids are happy, and even Pappy
Is proud as can be, though he's under the tree.

He's full of cheer (or is it beer?)
And chanting – avoiding Mommy's leer –
"Next year we're NOT WAITING 'til Christmas Eve
To assemble the toys. God help us, please."

FAVORITE SIGNS IN MY KITCHEN

"Help keep this kitchen clean – EAT OUT!"
Is a sign I find bewitchin'.
And "My wife wanted a new experience,
So I sent her to the kitchen."

"I run things around this house –
The vacuum, dishwasher, dryer – keep looking."
"This kitchen is closed, on account of illness –
The cook is sick of cooking."

"You have two choices for dinner tonight –
You can TAKE IT or LEAVE IT. Don't be nervous."
And, "This kitchen has its specialty – it is
Fast, friendly, efficient SELF-SERVICE."

I think the one I like the best
Is written on a spoon of wood –
"A clean house is a sign of a wasted life."
I'd print it in gold if I could.

MAIN QUALIFICATION

"I hear you just married, you son-of-a-gun.
Is she pretty?" He mumbled, "No."
"Does she have a good figure – stylish and smart?"
Once again he squirmed and said, "No."

"Does she have a great personality
Or is she a fantastic cook?"
He still answered "No" to each query
Which brought out a quizzical look.

"If she's not attractive or slim or smart,
And she's not a good cook and is sort of a sight,
Why on earth did you ever marry her?"
"Cuz SHE can still drive at night."

INSTANT PRIVACY

Two couples built a holiday cabin together
So they could share seashore vacations.
The structure was simple – just one large room.
They enjoyed it for years on many occasions.

"We've wondered how you have any privacy?"
And "How do you manage?" – both questions from locals.
"Well, when we were young we would pull sheets across,
But now that we're older, we remove our bifocals."

SENIORS AT THE WHEEL, BEWARE!

Some Florida Seniors have lost the art
Of driving down any main roads.
We're not as alert as we used to be
And we goof-up. Sometimes we're called "Toads."

Some of us wear two hearing aids
And many need glasses to drive.
Some gals use three pillows to see over the wheel –
Other heads can't turn from side to side.

But in spite of our ailments we NEED to drive
For the freedom to go our own way.
Can't be stuck at home when we need to roam,
So we drive, though we may swing and sway.

Many drive slowly in all the fast lanes.
This angers young drivers each day.
They pass us and gesture with their famous finger.
It's good we can't hear what they say.

The afternoon rush to Early Bird Specials
Is one of the worst, but we save a few dimes.
We've left cares behind – have one place in mind –
We're determined to meet the early deadlines.

There's a rumor that one group has started its own
Senior Citizen Airline called "High In The Sky."
They'll be flying soon, and their motto is this –
"You've seen us drive, now watch us fly."

We ask that young drivers have patience with us.
Just wave, honk or smile when you pass.
If you live long enough, you'll be like one of us
And YOU may be driving this way too. Alas!

SENIORS TALK ABOUT THEIR GRIPES

"One of the worst things about growing old,"
Said a Senior one day as he ate,
"Is getting food stuck in my teeth every meal.
It's annoying. It's something I hate."

"If you think that THAT'S the worst thing about aging,"
A friend said, "You're lucky as hell.
I'd trade my arthritis and aching knees
For food stuck in my teeth. I can tell."

"Putting my shoes on's the hardest thing
That I do all day long.
I've gained some weight. (Maybe something I ate?)
I don't bend in the middle. Guess that's what's wrong."

"Cutting toe nails is a rotten chore.
It must be done, but it's hard to do.
My arms are long but it's tough to twist
To reach my feet. I swear it's true."

"For me it's the stairs. They're hard to climb.
I KNOW that they build them steeper now.
Going down hurts my knees, but up is worse.
I avoid them whenever I can, somehow."

"I hear all your problems – have some of the same,
But for me the worst thing is NOT driving at night.
I'd give up a lot if my eyes weren't so dim
And I could have back some much better sight."

"You shouldn't complain! I can't drive at all!
The old meanies just took my license away.
I've lost independence – I'm so mad I could yell.
I have to ask *help* now to work or to play.

"My gripe is my face. It's so wrinkled and worn.
I hate to look into the mirror nowadays.
I don't know what happened. It used to be smooth.
Now it looks like a roadmap – a dry leather maze."

Cont. on next page

"Trying to get UP and OUT of a chair
Is such trouble. It's really a chore.
– Takes two or three tries to make it sometimes
Before I get up. I'm embarrassed! A bore."

"I've lost my hearing. It's worse each year.
My two hearing aids are not much help.
They magnify noise, not the human voice,
And I'm sick of their squealing and constant yelp."

"My feet are my problem. They really are sore.
I've corns and bunions and even a spur.
I walk with a wobble, and *also* I hobble.
A pair of new feet would make me purr."

"The thorn in my side is plain heartburn.
Whatever I eat turns to gas.
My stomach is bloated. My whole tongue is coated.
I can't even talk without burping. Alas!"

"If I had known that I'd live so long
I'd have taken much better care of myself.
I did everything wrong. I smoked – overate.
It's no wonder that soon I'll be put on the shelf."

A man said, "Let's all toss our cares in a ring,
Then *each* take one out from the pile."
You can guess what happened when all was finished.
Each one had retrieved his own with a smile.

There's a moral here somewhere, if truth be known.
No matter how hard our cross to bear
We prefer OUR problem to that of another.
Ours is familiar. We're coping with care.

So, let's not complain. It could be worse.
Let's hang in there still, and give it our BEST.
If we keep our chin up and try hard to smile,
It will help us survive – maybe even add ZEST.

GETTING READY FOR BED

"It sure takes longer to go to bed now,"
Said an elderly man to his friend.
"There are always so many chores to perform
I have to start early. It seems there's no end.

It takes a while to remove my clothes.
The worst thing is getting my shoes off (with ties.)
Then I soak and scrub and clean my dentures
And put eye drops in both my eyes.

I set the clock and remove my toupee.
Then hang my cane on the back of a chair
Before I unwind the elastic belt
That holds in my hernia, with a flair.

Then it's time to sit on the edge of the bed
And remove the bands on my knees.
Next I take off the pads on both of my corns
And also two bunions, if you please.

Next it's time to take off my glasses,
Then I think, *"Did I put out the cat?"*
After I take out both hearing aids
I'm deaf as a doornail and blind as a bat.

I crawl into bed really ready for sleep.
I've made it. I give three cheers.
I say my prayers and give my thanks
That I'm happy and healthy in spite of my years.

By now I am bushed, if I weren't before.
I reach and feel around for the lamp (ooh, a kink.)
But then I say, *It's not so bad*
*I still have my mind – **I think.***

STOP THAT BEAT! PLEASE!

Is rhythm a curse or a blessing, I wonder?
I can't decide which anymore.
There are times I just love it, but sometimes could shove it.
It depends where I am – either or.

It seems there is music wherever I go –
When I shop, when I bank, where I roam.
My fingers start snapping, my toes itch and twitch.
I'm embarrassed. I'd better go home.

Music is absolute murder in banks –
Formal ones, with ceilings so high
And stately, with floors made of oh-so-smooth marble
Just asking for dancing. Could die!

A grocery store's always my biggest downfall
With most aisles so long and so wide.
I cannot help waltzing and bowing down low
As I reach for the Cascade and Tide.

I sashay with flair down the tuna fish aisle.
I cha-cha near all frozen peas.
Why don't they just turn off the darned thing now
If we can't dance and prance as we please?

It's hard to control the great Big Band Sound.
Moonlight Serenade is the worst!
Most aisles are so wide they just tempt me to glide!
Shoppers stare and some glare. I could burst!

There's very strong pulsating rhythm and beat
As I take some more food from the shelf.
Then I give up and say, "Oh, to heck with it now,"
And just dance away all by myself.

Cont. on next page

Oh curses! They're playing a tango now.
I'd better lean hard on my cart.
But soon I'm overcome by the beat "Dah-dee-dum"
And I slink five long strides like a tart.

Next I swing and I sway with dear Sammy Kaye
On aisles that just ask to be used.
I twirl, then add dips, as I reach for the chips.
Shoppers both are confused and amused.

I can never resist the Mariachi band beat
Of Mexico. Trumpets so gay
And violins adding their fine fiddle flair.
Soon I'm off and line dancing. Olé!

Country Western's neat beat's irresistible.
What fun. I now scoot with some hoots.
I side-kick and stomp as I circle away.
I really should have on my boots.

Oh, no. I've drawn a big audience nearby.
They're clapping in time to the beat.
I kneel down to reach the unreachable bleach,
Then I curtsey to give them a treat.

I'm sunk. Now they're playing a smooth Bosa Nova.
The rhythm is going through my skin.
I hum with the dum-dee-dum beat of the drum
As I grab cheddar cheese from the bin.

The Charleston's an all-time favorite of mine.
Sheer rapture must show on my face.
I pile in the Oreos and crackers with glee
While striving to move with some grace.

Cont. on next page

Caribbean steel bands are at times my undoing
With metallic sounds flowing and loud.
My whole body melts as mellifluous tunes play.
Oh, help! Now I'm drawing a crowd.

A Bolero just kicked in. I'm a goner for sure.
Where oh where are the candied orange peels?
I just can't be sedate with provocative beat
So I give up and kick up my heels.

I don't believe this! Oh, shades of my youth!
They're playing Spike Jones and his Cowbell solo.
I laughed at it then, and it's still funny now.
I toss beans in my cart from way down below.

The Foxtrot now builds to crescendo so loud.
No wonder my blood's pumping fast.
The beat throbs my head with excitement galore.
How long can I hold out, or last?

I'm making a dumb, utter fool of myself.
A Samba just started. That's fine –
'Til it hits me, "What an ideal place it is here
For a long, winding, fun Congo line."

Tommy Dorsey is playing his sweet slide trombone.
What memories and joys it brings back.
I feel sentimental as I choose bars of soap.
When he slides, I slide – there's no slack.

I'm sunk when guitar music strums out Hawaiian
'Cuz shopping requires both hands.
I feel everything jiggle – my hips start to wiggle –
It's almost as bad as Big Bands.

Cont. next page

A passerby just called me "Miss Twinkle Toes."
I'm choosing desserts – sherbet ice would be nice.
I study my grocery list, still pretty long.
I need to get pasta and rice.

My partner's my cart – together we dart
In time to the rhythms that reach to the sky.
Why can't I stand still? Why must I still thrill
To the music of days long gone by?

Some people get by without changing their walk.
They merely give fingers a snap.
I envy their coolness and grace under fire.
With me, still, my toes gotta tap.

You'd think at my age I could now simmer down
And at least just ignore any jive.
But the record spins on, and until I'm gone
I'll just dance. It makes me come alive.

In my dotage I've now solved the problem so big.
Though some people surely will scoff.
When rhythmical music is too much to bear
I just turn both my hearing aids off.

HALLELUJAH! I'M RETIRING!

Today's the day that I retire!
No more neckties now for me.
Forget starched shirts that scratch my neck
Or pants with creases for all to see.

There'll be no need to set the clock.
I can sleep late if I please.
I might not ever shave again!
For this I give thanks on my knees.

There'll be no taking orders.
I'll do only what I wish.
I can watch the soaps or late night shows,
Or I can just go fish.

No need to wait for weekends
To play a game of golf,
Or sail in my Sun Fish,
Or read or just goof-off.

The future sure looks rosy.
"Mind-boggling" is the word.
Twenty-four hours to do as I wish.
From now on I'm as free as a bird.

I'm wondering how my wife will take it.
There's one little thing that bothers me.
She volunteers, plays bridge, line dances.
Will she have time to play with me?

She gave me an electric can-opener,
A case of soup and chips to munch.
Said, "I married you for better or worse, but
that does NOT include lunch."

TIMES CHANGE AND SO DO PEOPLE
(My lovely friend and neighbor told this story on herself)

Her six year old grandchild was visiting my friend
When she noticed a photo on the bedroom chest.
"Who is that beautiful lady?" she asked.
"She looks like a movie star. One of the best!"

"Oh, that picture was taken when I was in college,
Far, far away, and a long time ago."
The child was speechless. Her mouth opened wide.
"That picture was YOU, Gram? You really say so?"

She looked at the photo, then back to her grandma.
She scrutinized both again and again.
She could not believe they were one and the same,
Then she finally asked, "What happened? And when?"

A HAPPY RETIREE

The gold watch was given, the speeches were made,
The well-wishers said their adieus.
He'd worked in the office for forty-five years
Doing a good job and paying his dues.

"What plans do you have for the rest of your life?"
A fellow co-worker asked Jo.
"I've got me a cabin in Maine on the water.
I'll watch the fish jump, and lie low."

Jo murmured, "For six months I'm jes gonna set
In my rocker, on my porch, at the lake in Dunockin."
"Do you know what you'll do after six months have passed?"
"Sure, that's easy, 'cuz then I'll start rockin' "

HOW I DECIDED WHERE TO RETIRE

A New England blizzard left three feet of snow
Just after I'd shoveled for days and days.
I finally decided I'd had enough!
I was tired of living in a snow-white daze.

I'm going to retire where I don't have to lift
Again one more shovelful of snow.
I'll get in my car and head South every day
'Til I finally decide where to go.

I took my snow shovel and at each gas stop
I stood it along side my car.
People would say, "That's a great snow shovel."
I'd get back in my car and drive far.

This happened in every state down the coast.
I'd stand up my shovel and wait.
People kept saying, "That's a great snow shovel."
I'd soon make a bee-line for the next state.

When I reached Florida and was getting gas
I stood up the snow shovel to see "what gives?"
When all of the people asked, "What is THAT?"
I KNEW I had found where I want to live.

HELP! MY HUSBAND HAS RETIRED!

Having a husband around the house
All day and also all night
Has changed my life considerably
I must get dressed. Can't look a fright.

It's hard to vacuum around a man
Who's lounging in his lounge chair.
And dirty dishes in the sink
Are driving me to despair.

I need to arm-wrestle to get the phone.
He uses it for hours –
He calls stock brokers, Medicare,
Insurance companies and other powers.

He studies reports in his Wall Street Journal
While I'm in the kitchen preparing a meal.
He visits with friends in the driveway daily
While I'm making beds and cleaning. Some deal!

The way he's dressed he looks a mess
And what is worse, he refuses to shave.
This retirement has really gone to his head.
I think he's forgotten how to behave.

I may as well resign myself
Though I'm too upset for words.
His retirement for him is great.
For me it's for the birds.

His constant questions are driving me crazy.
"What's for dinner?" and "What's up, honey?"
For him retirement's fun, but for me
It's twice as much husband and half as much money.

WHAT'S IN A NAME

We elders are called by many names
Some of them are not repeatable.
But we're hanging in there and doing our best
With spirits sky high and unbeatable.

In the South we are called "Senior Citizens."
It's dignified, but it sounds so cold.
In London they say, "We ARE getting on."
Whatever they call us, we hate the word "old."

In the Midwest they say we are "Over-The-Hill,"
But considering the alternative, who cares? We've managed.
In Vermont we're like cheese – "The older the better."
They say , "We're chronologically advantaged."

Whatever we're called, we're worth lots of money.
Our hair's full of silver, and teeth filled with gold.
Our stomachs have gas, and our kidneys have stones.
Our feet feel like lead, but does that mean we're old?

It's true our joints crack when we bend.
We need glasses to help our dim eyes.
And our knees go out "oftener" than we do,
But for trying, we all get a prize.

We love going for Early Bird Specials.
Seniors! 10% off! Won't embellish.
We're all on that new seafood diet –
We see food and we eat it, with relish.

Complaining's *verboten* for most of us.
We try not to mention our new ache or pain –
Just suffer in silence if needed
Even though our bones tell us it's soon going to rain.

Some of us need a wake-up call
Even though we are wide awake.
But please don't rain on our parade
And ignore us, for heaven's sake.

Cont. on next page

They tell us to keep our powder dry –
Not-to-worry. Don't fret. Just hang loose.
That's easy to say, but once in a while
Our ends drag and sag, just like a caboose.

We all have a similar, horrible problem –
We cannot remember from here to there.
But with hearing aids squealing and eyes dripping tears
We keep going, all the time we are losing our hair.

We make ourselves get out of bed in the morning
And smile a while before we eat.
We mainline our vitamins daily to have
Lots of vigor and vim. No small feat.

It haunts us so much that we lose things.
"I just HAD it. It was HERE. What the heck."
We hunt and we hunt for our glasses that
We finally find hanging around our neck.

It's true that time goes fast when you're having fun.
But even if not, it speeds by.
Most of us say we don't want to *rust* out.
So we *wear* out instead while we fly.

We're told we must use it or lose it
So we exercise. "Shape up. Be fit."
But parts of our body tell us to slow down
Sometimes 'cuz our anchor is draggin' a bit.

We know not to stop half way up on the stairs, or
We'll say, "Am I going up or heading down right now?"
Our age may concern us but one thing we know –
We can't be any younger than we are right now.

At least we are trying to lead the good life –
Attend church – don't hang out in bars.
We all volunteer, write letters of cheer,
So whatever you call us, we SHOULD get GOLD STARS.

INTERVIEWING SENIOR SENIOR CITIZENS
(Some of their answers bring a smile)

A reporter was interviewing elderly people
In a Senior Home one noon.
"What did you have for breakfast today?"
"A bowl of bran, Metamucil and prunes."

"Is there a man in your life to keep you warm?"
The reporter teased a Miss Cranket.
"No, there's no man to warm me at night –
Only an electric blanket."

"What do you do for excitement?" she asked
A chipper elder named Clempty.
"I get in my flivver and see how far
I can drive the derned thing on empty."

"And what do you think of growing old?"
She asked a spry Senior named Kate.
"When you consider the alternative,
Growing older is really great."

"Do you exercise to stay so fit?"
Asked the interviewer, with a word in edgewise.
"No, my exercise is acting as pallbearer
For all my friends who exercise."

She asked a woman who smiled a lot
If she is happy when she wakes up.
"Of course I wake up happy because
I'm happy that I woke up."

"You look so tired. Are you alright?"
She asked a gal who was barely sewing.
"I can tell you just how zapped I am –
I can't even get this rocking chair going.

Cont. on next page

"If you could pick the way you would die,"
She asked Joe, "Do you know how it would be?"
"I'd like to be shot by a jealous husband
At the ripe old age of one hundred and three."

The reporter asked a man now celebrating
His one hundredth birthday – a vet, well-met.
"Please tell – have you lived in this town all your life?"
He winked, then answered, "Almost, but not yet."

SYMPHONIC HUMOR

I was twelve when I heard my first symphony concert
In lovely Minneapolis, Minnesota.
It was memorable, and unforgettable, too,
Worth driving for from South Dakota.

The great conductor, Eugene Normandy,
Was in rare, fine form, for certain,
When an incident happened I'll never forget
That nearly brought down the curtain.

The music climbed to a rousing crescendo –
Then a cut-off. Deafening silence was jarred
By a very loud voice from the audience shouting,
"Ve frry ourss in LARD!"

Everyone roared! The conductor turned
And performed an exaggerated very low bow.
Then, what he said brought the house down again,
"Madam, may I have your recipe, now?"

The symphony audiences I've been part of since then
Have been proper, correct and so right.
But thus far none's equaled the fun of that loud
Swedish voice in the still of the night.

ODE TO MY LOVE
ON OUR 50TH WEDDING ANNIVERSARY

We were married in a blizzard
Fifty years ago today,
In a South Dakota storm so fierce
The groom was late that day.

Willard and both his brothers
Limped in on the same caboose.
Though sad was our fate that they were a day late,
In a blizzard you have to hang loose.

Instead of the morning the wedding took place
In the evening. It really was late.
But my parents were happy, especially my Pappy –
The announcements still had the right date.

God sent us a baby boy named Jack,
Soon followed by his brother Bill.
And later came along the third,
A little girl named Jill.

They brought us joy and happiness.
All three made us very proud.
If you will just sit still a bit
I'll wax eloquently and loud.

They married super partners
So we added to the fold
Two daughters fair, and one new son –
Three more to have and hold.

They've blessed us in so many ways
On earth instead of heaven.
Now they have children we both love –
Grandchildren – lucky seven.

Cont. on next page

Like famous Martin Luther King
My husband had a dream
To build a house all by himself –
A most unlikely scheme!

He. hadn't shared this dream with me
Before the wedding bell,
Or I'd have had the chance right then
To tell him to "Go to ____!"

His dream became my nightmare
As we drove to Vermont each weekend.
We packed, unpacked, we shoveled and picked
Until our poor backs were weakened.

We looked like the Oakies when driving
With lumber tied on. 'Twas no lark.
We often were called "The Night Riders"
As we snuck out of town in the dark.

"Slave Labor Camp In The Frozen North"
Is the name I called the spot.
It took us so long to build it not wrong
That I thought the first part would rot.

But proof that some miracles really exist,
Though I cannot tell you why,
"The Vermontclair Palace" has finally emerged
From cocoon to butterfly.

It's now a neat home with plumbing,
Walls of glass, doors and huge decks –
Electricity and appliances,
What will they think of next?

So Willard now is vindicated.
The ski house is his dream come true.
I have to admit his idea was good,
And give the devil his due.

Cont. on next page

For thirty-seven years we lived
In beautiful Upper Montclair.
Our home was happy, lively and filled
With family, friends, fun – our own lair.

But when Willard retired we headed south
Near beaches, sun, golf – our new turf
Is on a canal that we both adore.
We call it our "Heaven on Earth."

The wildlife of Florida
Is right at our front door.
Great blue herons, tall white egrets
Fat brown pelicans and more.

Willard has fun on his
Fourteen foot yacht
Taking grandchildren fishing –
They like it a LOT.

We love to greet our visitors
Who flee the cold weather and strife
With a hug and a kiss, and then we don't miss,
"Welcome to Paradise and the Good Life."

We're blessed with many friends we love
Both old ones as well as new.
We treasure each and every one. They color
Our lives a beautiful hue.

We've traveled the globe to
North, South, East and West,
But we're hard pressed to tell you
What place we like best.

We've climbed to the top for the view at most places,
We visited castles, cathedrals galore.
We drove on the wrong side, rode donkeys and camels,
Walked miles in museums, seen sights, and much more.

Cont. on next page

We know we were born to be tourists.
Have flight bags – will travel – can roam.
Just show us a colorful brochure,
And our feet start to itch to leave home.

We're happy as clams and busy as bees
On the run both day and night.
When others admonish, "You MUST slow down!"
We tell them to "Go fly a kite."

We called it a rat race
Of duties, before,
But now it's a whirlwind
With pleasures in store.

Some people have asked for a recipe
For a marriage to last fifty years.
"Just stick it out through thick and thin
Amid both laughter and tears."

He gripes, I nag, we argue, and then
We kiss and make up, and start over again.
At least we communicate often and loudly
So our marriage is happy. We wear our badge proudly.

We're still burning the candles at both ends
And it makes such a beautiful light.
We know that we're lucky – we'll try to be plucky
If old age catches up in the night.

We were married in a blizzard
Only fifty years ago
And from where I sit, (or lie, or stand)
All systems still are "GO!"

All My Love,

Marguerite
Your slave (driver)

February 11, 1989

Nov, Marguerite Loucks Dye
4715 Mt. Vernon Drive
Bradenton, FL 34210
MAY

JUNE Marguerite Loucks Dye
RR Box 3162
Killington, VT 05751
OCT.

80.